About the Author

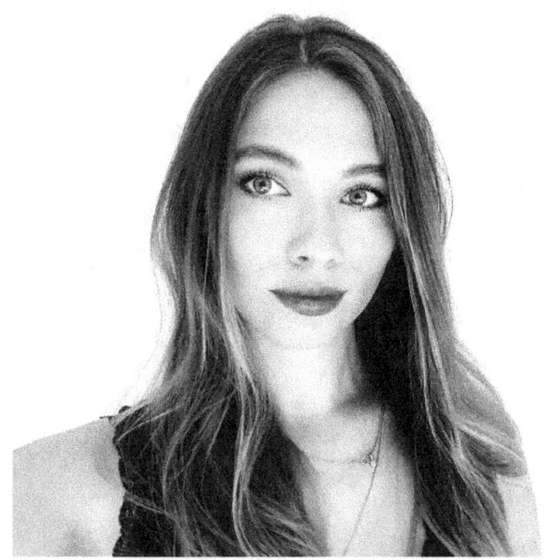

Elena Stepkina is a distinguished artist, psychologist, art therapist, and entrepreneur based in New York, USA. She is a member of the International Union of Teacher Artists, the Russian Association of Art Therapists, and the Eurasian Art Union.

Officially recognized as extraordinary, Elena received a talent visa to the United States in 2022, underscoring her exceptional skills and contributions to the fields of art and therapy.

In a remarkably short period of six months, Elena established a gallery in the heart of Manhattan and successfully organized seven international exhibitions.

Her artistic prowess was previously acknowledged through a personal exhibition at the Tretyakov Gallery, Russia's premier gallery.

Elena's academic background is extensive, with four degrees in design, management, psychology, and art therapy.

Her work in art therapy has been widely published, with articles appearing in over 80 countries, as well as in scientific journals included in the Russian Science Citation Index (RSCI) and the Higher Attestation Commission (HAC).

Since 2012, she has been actively involved in creative work with children in orphanages, implementing over 50 projects aimed at fostering creativity and emotional well-being.

Her expertise has also seen her serve as a judge at prestigious international competitions. Furthermore, she teaches art therapy to international students in various global projects.

Elena's creative achievements have gained international recognition. She is a silver medalist in the British international painting competition "Golden Time Talent" and the Spanish international painting competition "Dali's Mustache." She is also a member of the international chamber JCI, having previously served as vice president for social projects.

Elena Stepkina's career is marked by a unique blend of artistic excellence and therapeutic impact, making her a prominent figure in the global art and art therapy community. This book aims to share the results of Elena's scientific work in the field.

STUDY OF THE INFLUENCE OF ART THERAPY ON THE FORMATION OF THE INTERNAL SUPPORT OF THE PERSONALITY

Author: Elena Ivanovna Stepkina

Affiliations: Member of the International Union of Teacher Artists, Member of the Russian Association of Art Therapists, Member of the Eurasian Art Union, Artist, Psychologist, Art Therapist, Individual Entrepreneur.

New York, USA

Summary:

This study investigates the impact of self-administered art therapy exercises on participants. The experiment involved individuals who expressed concerns such as anxiety, uncertainty, and chronic stress. The participants underwent initial testing and were provided with a set of art therapy exercises in written format along with a suggested timeline for completion. After three weeks, the participants were retested without access to their previous responses. The results demonstrated improvements in all five criteria assessed during the testing process, highlighting the positive effects of engaging in art therapy exercises on participants' well-being.

Keywords: art therapy, psychology, testing, research, exercises, independent work, anxiety, stress, nervous tension, fatigue, lack of stability, fear, psychologist, help, performance improvement.

The relevance of this research lies in the fact that the issue of emotional support and reliance on one's personal qualities has become increasingly acute in the current economic and social instability of society. Almost every individual is constantly experiencing anxiety, stress, and uncertainty, which they need to manage on a daily basis.

According to psychologists, there has been an increase in the number of people displaying heightened anxiety and emotional instability in recent years. Consequently, addressing emotional disturbances and timely correction have become highly relevant. Modern medicine affirms that 30-40% of chronic illnesses have a psychogenic basis. Therefore, it is crucial to consider how to maintain both physical and psychological health in contemporary conditions.

Since 2019, psychologists have noted an increase in patients seeking support due to a lack of emotional stability. Given the current global situation, seeking external support is practically impossible, making the development of internal support highly effective.

Art therapy is increasingly being utilized by psychologists as a universal and non-intrusive method of interacting with clients for the psychological correction of emotional stability disturbances. The significance of this study is thus underscored by the rapid growth in the number of individuals experiencing emotional disorders and the urgent need for corrective work in the formation of internal support through art therapy, which has immense potential. Art therapy has established itself as a highly effective and minimally intrusive approach.

Despite the increased demand for psychological assistance, insufficient attention is given to the formation of individuals' internal support and their personal qualities. Often, psychologists focus on situational issues, while art therapy offers an opportunity for in-depth problem exploration. Furthermore, the current research disregards the role of the art therapist's personality. All participants in the study solely follow the textual instructions without the therapist's involvement.

The object of the study is the process of forming internal support in individuals using art therapy methods without therapist participation.

The subject of the study is the formation of internal support in individuals through the application of art therapy methods.

The research aims to adapt art therapy methods to the task of developing internal support for the participants.

To achieve this goal, the following tasks are to be accomplished:

1. Establish a clear understanding of the criteria that constitute the concept of "personality."

2. Examine the specificity of art therapy as a method in psychotherapy.

3. Determine the potential of applying art therapy methods for developing internal support in individuals.

4. Prepare a comprehensive set of art therapy exercises aimed at developing internal support for clients.

5. Conduct an experimental study with a control group.

6. Collect and analyze the results.

7. Draw conclusions from the conducted work.

The research hypothesis suggests that by designing a series of art therapy exercises focused on creating internal support in individuals and applying them in practice, an increase in the indicators of internal support and a decrease in stress and anxiety levels can be observed among the control group. The research methods include theoretical analysis and synthesis of literature related to the research problem, empirical methods such as testing and experiments, and mathematical methods for data analysis.

The experimental base of the study consists of men and women aged 25 to 40 who are employed and have sought or expressed a desire to seek psychological assistance due to nervous tension and anxiety related to the lack of stability in their lives. The practical significance of this research lies in the obtained data and the developed corrective program, which can be utilized by psychologists and art therapists. The research findings can be valuable in the development of methodological recommendations for educators, psychologists, caregivers, and parents. Moreover, they can benefit individuals seeking to enhance their internal support.

Based on the aforementioned, it can be reasonably presumed that art therapy is effective in fostering internal support. The sessions significantly reduce anxiety and stress levels while strengthening the nervous system. An empirical study investigating the influence of art therapy on the formation of internal support in individuals has been conducted.

The aim of the empirical study is to investigate the correlation between engaging in art therapy sessions and the increase in individuals' internal support for themselves. The hypothesis posits that art therapy methods are an effective means of developing internal support. To achieve the research objective and validate the hypothesis, the following tasks have been formulated:

- Select psychodiagnostic methods aligned with the research objectives.

- Develop a program for fostering internal support using art therapy techniques.

- Conduct an empirical study and track the dynamics of the measured indicators.

The study will be conducted online, considering the increasing digitization of the modern world. Creating a safe online environment will help participants experience the digital realm as secure, open, ecologically friendly, and therapeutic.

A total of 32 participants, comprising 27 women and 5 men, have been recruited for the study. They have expressed concerns related to anxiety, uncertainty, the changing world, internal support, and the state of ambiguity.

Participants will undergo an initial assessment to establish a baseline. Over the course of three weeks, they will engage in art therapy tasks, respond to questions, and provide feedback after completing each task. At the end of the three-week period, a follow-up assessment will be conducted to evaluate any changes.

Conducting the Research Testing In order to assess the participants' initial state and evaluate their progress after completing the program, a test was developed. Participants are required to rate their current state on a 10-point scale for each question.

Test Questions:

1. Rate your level of anxiety (0 - not anxious at all, 10 - constantly experiencing feelings of anxiety).

2. Do you have any sleep problems? (0 - no problems, 10 - disrupted sleep schedule and poor sleep quality).

3. How strongly do you feel supported by your loved ones? (0 - no support, 10 - complete support).

4. How fulfilled do you feel in life? (0 - not fulfilled, 10 - completely fulfilled).

5. Do you experience fear of the unknown? (0 - no fear, confidently embrace the new, 10 - new experiences greatly frighten me).

Table of Participants' Responses.

	Your Gender	1. Rate your level of anxiety	2. Do you have sleep problems?	5. Do you have fear of the unknown?	Sum LOWER is better	3. How strongly do you feel support from loved ones?	4. How fulfilled do you feel in life?	Sum HIGHER is better
1	M	7	9	2	18	10	7	17
2	F	7	4	5	16	10	6	16
3	M	7	2	5	14	8	7	15
4	F	10	4	6	20	6	0	6
5	F	5	5	8	18	0	10	10
6	F	8	10	1	19	9	8	17
7	F	7	8	8	23	4	3	7
8	F	8	10	4	22	4	4	8
9	F	10	0	9	19	8	5	13
10	F	6	10	6	22	10	9	19
11	F	7	7	4	18	5	4	9
12	F	6	10	10	26	5	3	8
13	F	8	7	8	23	9	6	15
14	F	6	8	6	20	5	4	9
15	F	7	7	6	20	10	5	15
16	M	5	7	3	15	3	7	10
17	F	6	3	9	18	8	7	15
18	F	7	5	6	18	4	5	9
19	F	8	2	9	19	6	5	11
20	F	6	8	6	20	4	8	12
21	F	10	8	8	26	6	3	9
22	F	7	6	4	17	7	8	15
23	F	10	10	7	27	0	5	5
24	F	9	1	8	18	4	3	7
25	F	9	9	9	27	10	10	20
26	F	7	5	7	19	9	5	14
27	F	8	3	9	20	9	6	15
28	M	6	4	7	17	8	5	13
29	F	7	8	6	21	7	6	13
30	M	6	4	5	15	7	6	13
31	F	6	5	7	18	9	8	17
32	F	8	10	2	20	8	8	16
Total:		234	199	200	633	212	186	398

The table presents the results of the initial survey of the participants. Additionally, the sums for the first three questions and the last two questions have been calculated. A lower sum for the first three questions and a higher sum for the last two indicate a more harmonious and stable personality.

Now let's present the participants' responses to each question in a graphical format.

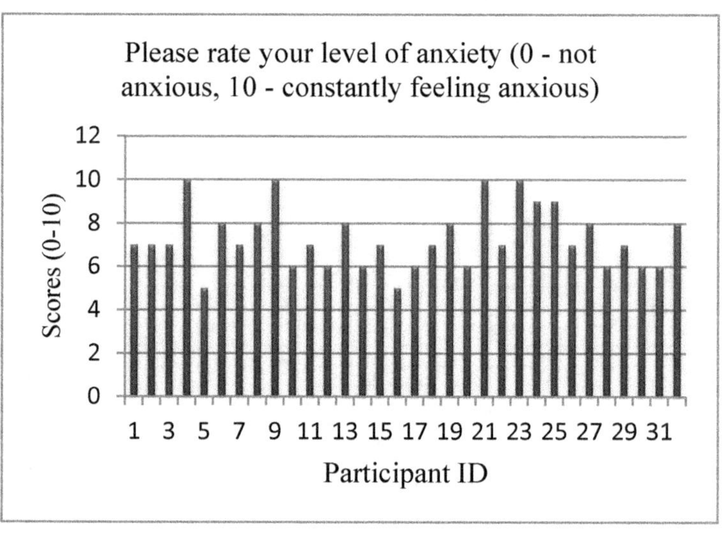

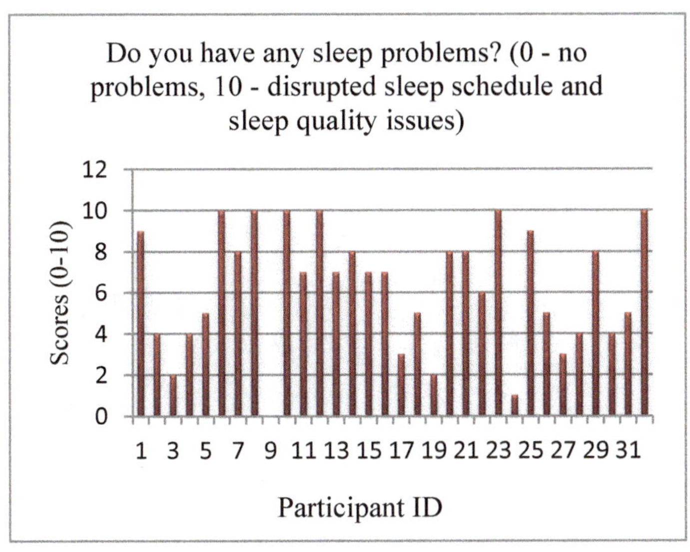

Do you have any sleep problems? (0 - no problems, 10 - disrupted sleep schedule and sleep quality issues)

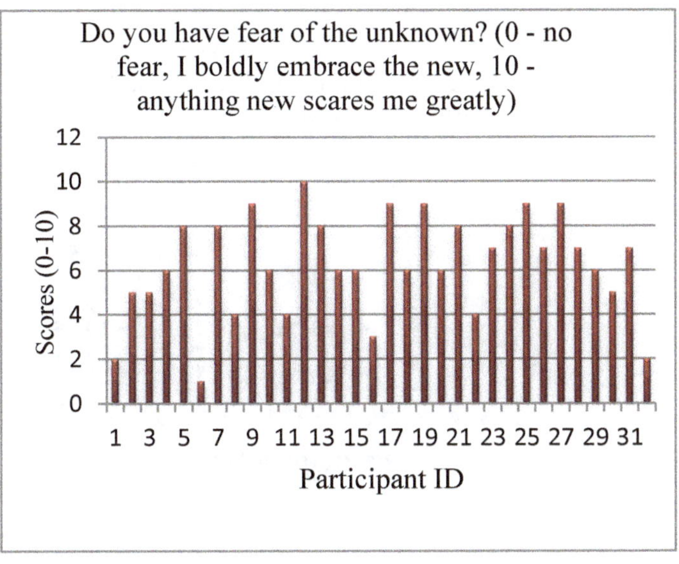

Do you have fear of the unknown? (0 - no fear, I boldly embrace the new, 10 - anything new scares me greatly)

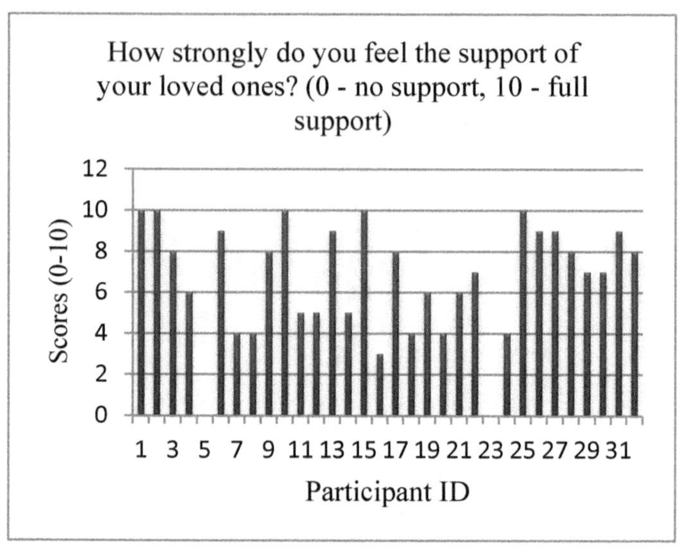

How strongly do you feel the support of your loved ones? (0 - no support, 10 - full support)
Scores (0-10)
12
10
8
6
4
2
0
1 3 5 7 9 11 13 15 17 19 21 23 25 27 29 31
Participant ID

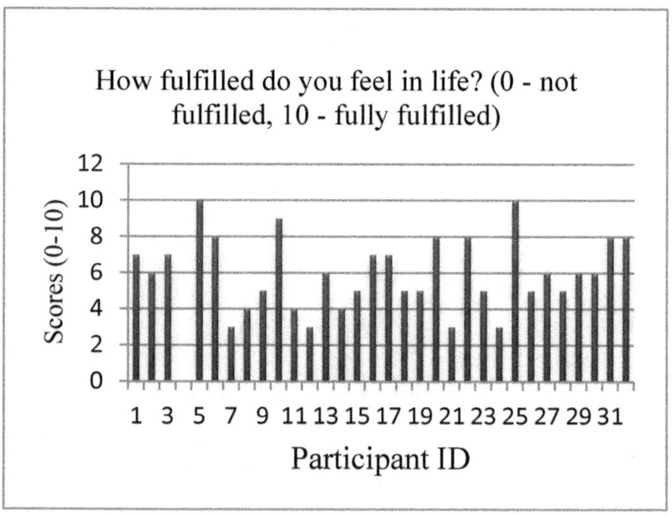

How fulfilled do you feel in life? (0 - not fulfilled, 10 - fully fulfilled)
Scores (0-10)
12
10
8
6
4
2
0
1 3 5 7 9 11 13 15 17 19 21 23 25 27 29 31
Participant ID

Now let's compare the average scores, minimum scores, and maximum scores for each question.

	Question 1 (Anxiety)	Question 2 (Sleep)	Question 3 (Uncertainty)	Question 4 (Support)	Question 5 (Fulfillment)
Minimum Value	5	0	1	0	0
Maximum Value	10	10	10	10	10
Sum	234	199	200	212	186
Mean Value	7,3	6,2	6,3	6,6	5,8

For ease of perception, columns where the best indicator is the minimum value are highlighted in blue, and where the maximum value is the maximum value are highlighted in pink. From this summary table, we can draw the following conclusions:

1.   The question about anxiety has the maximum value in the blue column.

2.   The minimum value in the anxiety question is 5, considering that the scale starts from 0.

3.	Sleep seems to be in a better condition. However, the average value indicates that the majority of respondents experience difficulties with sleep.

4.	Uncertainty scares a significant portion of the participants.

5.	More than half of the participants feel supported. However, as can be seen from the graph, two individuals marked 0 in this item.

6.	One person responded with 0 to the question about fulfillment.

7.	On average, the fulfillment value is relatively low, indicating more of a lack of fulfillment rather than a satisfactory result. Since the respondents were in the age range of 25-40, a value of 5.8 suggests a lack of fulfillment.

Afterward, participants were provided with detailed written descriptions of the tasks, as well as a rough schedule for completing these tasks. For the exercises, all participants prepared A4-sized sheets of paper, a thin black marker, and paints (tempera/acrylic).

Detailed description of exercises and instructions for their implementation.

"Inside Yourself"

Draw a large circle on a sheet of paper using any color. Do not fill it in. The circle represents you. Now think about the difficult situations and problems that surround you. Think about what can "throw you off track" or simply upset you. Choose one event at a time, assign a color to it, and draw it outside the boundaries of the circle. You can choose any shape - a brushstroke, a circle, a square, something sharp, etc. The size and number of events are determined based on your preference.

After that, think about the events that bring you joy, provide support, and make you feel better. There are no limitations here. Simply choose what you like and draw these events inside the circle. Just like in the first case, you can choose any shape.

After completing these actions, look at the circle symbolizing you and consider whether you want to strengthen your boundaries so that unwanted events cannot penetrate inside the circle. If you feel the desire, you can reinforce them by outlining them with a thicker line or multiple lines.

Now look at the resulting drawing. Inside you, there are only positive events. They fill you up and make you strong. External events can be anything - they cannot penetrate inside; they are only on the outside and cannot harm you. What other conclusions can you draw from this exercise?

"Release"

Exercise for anger. If you feel angry and powerless, be sure to perform this exercise.

Take several sheets of A4-sized paper and a marker. Place a sheet of paper in front of you and take the marker. Think about a situation that causes anger and powerlessness. Feel this situation with your entire body. When you feel that the emotion has reached its peak, start vigorously scribbling on the paper with the marker, releasing all your emotions. Just transfer your anger and despair onto the paper with all your strength. If this is not enough, take a second or third sheet of paper. If you feel like it, you can crumple or tear the scribbled sheets. Continue this exercise until you run out of energy. One exercise per situation. If there are many similar situations, work on each one separately.

"The Strength Poster"

Exercise for acknowledging your achievements and building internal support.

To perform this exercise, you will need a large sheet of paper, preferably drawing paper, and drawing tools. If you don't have drawing tools, a regular black marker will suffice. Now, on the sheet of paper, draw circles and write your achievements in the center of each circle. The circles can vary in size and be placed randomly on the paper. It is crucial to remember two things: firstly, write down all your achievements, even the smallest ones, and secondly, continue this exercise throughout the three weeks and keep the "poster of strength" in a visible place so that you can see what you have already accomplished. It is even better to constantly add new achievements to it.

"Letting Go"

Often, there are situations that we are unable to change or have any influence on, yet we constantly think about them and waste our energy creating incredible scenarios in our heads. You will need a sheet of A3 or A4 paper, paints, or a simple marker for this exercise.

Draw a small figure of yourself at the bottom of the paper, around 2-3 cm in height. Then, at the top of the paper, draw balloons without strings. Just balloons. Draw 2 to 5 balloons, depending on the number of situations you want to let go of. Now, inside each balloon, write down the situations that drain your energy but are beyond your control. Some balloons may remain empty, or you can add more if needed. After completing this, take a thin marker or pencil and intentionally draw the strings. If you realize that you are unable to let go of a particular situation at the moment, draw a string connected to the person. If you feel that you want to release a situation, that it has served its purpose, and you have done everything you could, confidently draw a short, free-hanging string as a sign that the balloon and everything related to that situation will fly away forever.

Monitor your emotions immediately after the exercise and also after a couple of days. Look at the drawing again and become aware of how your attitude has changed towards the "released" balloons.

"Self-Portraits"

This exercise should be done consistently. Over the course of the three weeks, you need to collect at least five photos where you are genuinely smiling. Where it is evident from the photos that you are happy. Put these photos in an envelope. In moments of sadness or self-doubt, take out these photos and look at them. It is essential that these are physical photographs, not images on a phone screen.

While looking at the photos, try to be aware that it is you. You are this person - smiling and happy. Tell yourself, "Yes, this is who I am." How does it make you feel?

"Breathing"

During moments of nervous tension or anxiety (or while recalling these moments), our breathing is often disrupted. Therefore, it is important to perform an exercise to restore our breathing rhythm, which will help calm down and return to normal. You will need a sheet of A4 paper and any writing tool (marker, pen, pencil). Your task is to count, breathe, and draw simultaneously.

Place the marker in the lower left corner (0.5 cm away from the edges), and on the inhale, counting slowly "one, two," draw a straight line upward, parallel to the left edge of the paper. Now count "three, four," and draw a line to the right, parallel to it, as you exhale. Then, on the next inhale count, draw a line downward, and on the exhale, count to complete the cycle. This is only the first circle.

Now start drawing a rectangular spiral, which means doing the same but half a centimeter closer to the center of the paper. After three or four repetitions, try to take one inhale for a full circle and one exhale for the next. Keep drawing, counting, and breathing until you realize that besides breathing and counting, there is nothing else in your mind.

This is an excellent and highly effective way to calm down in any situation.

"Sorting it Out"

Often, our minds become cluttered, especially during studying or before an exam. But this exercise is also effective for those who simply experience a mix of a million thoughts swirling in their heads. You will need three sheets of paper and a marker. On the first sheet, draw the chaos that is happening inside your head. Just a tangle of lines. There are no rules - draw as you feel. After you've finished drawing, observe your thoughts and feelings. Now, it's time to untangle it. Take the second sheet and draw straight horizontal lines parallel to the edge of the paper. It's as if you're creating a text, but instead of letters, use lines. How do you feel now? Take the third sheet and draw shelves. Small, thin rectangles or just lines - it's up to you. With the marker, "place" your thoughts and knowledge on the shelves in the form of books. Draw book spines on the shelves. You can color them, number them, or give them titles, both for the books and the shelves themselves (e.g., social media marketing on one shelf, cooking on another).

What emotions do you feel after organizing all your thoughts on the shelves?

Next, a schedule of art therapy exercises was developed, which the participants followed for three weeks. It is not a strict requirement but simply helps participants to know when to perform which exercises.

Additionally, each participant can apply any exercise situationally.

	Monday	Tuesday	Wednesday	Thursday	Friday	Saturday	Sunday
Week 1	Release	Release		Breathing	Inside Yourself		Breathing
Week 2		Sorting it Out		Strength Poster		This is Me	
Week 3	Strength Poster		This is Me		Sorting it Out	Letting Go	Letting Go

After three weeks of independent practice of the exercises, the participants were asked the same questions again. They did not see their previous answers.

Subsequently, a summary analysis was conducted comparing the initial answers and the answers after completing the course. The answers provided before taking the course are highlighted in red, while the ones given after are highlighted in green.

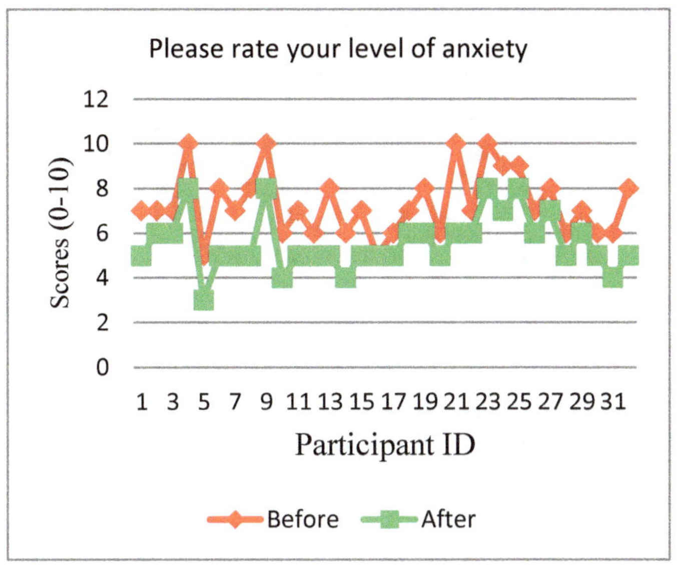

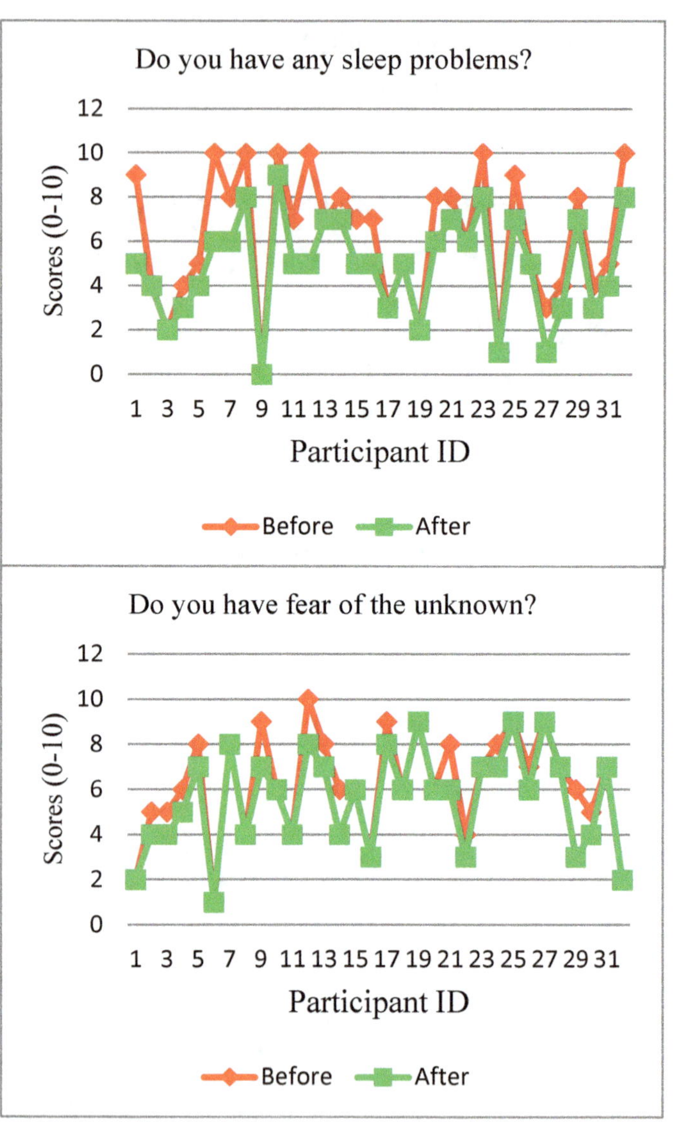

Do you have any sleep problems?
Scores (0-10)
12
10
8
6
4
2
0
1 3 5 7 9 11 13 15 17 19 21 23 25 27 29 31
Participant ID
Before
After
Do you have fear of the unknown?
Scores (0-10)
12
10
8
6
4
2
0
1 3 5 7 9 11 13 15 17 19 21 23 25 27 29 31
Participant ID
Before
After

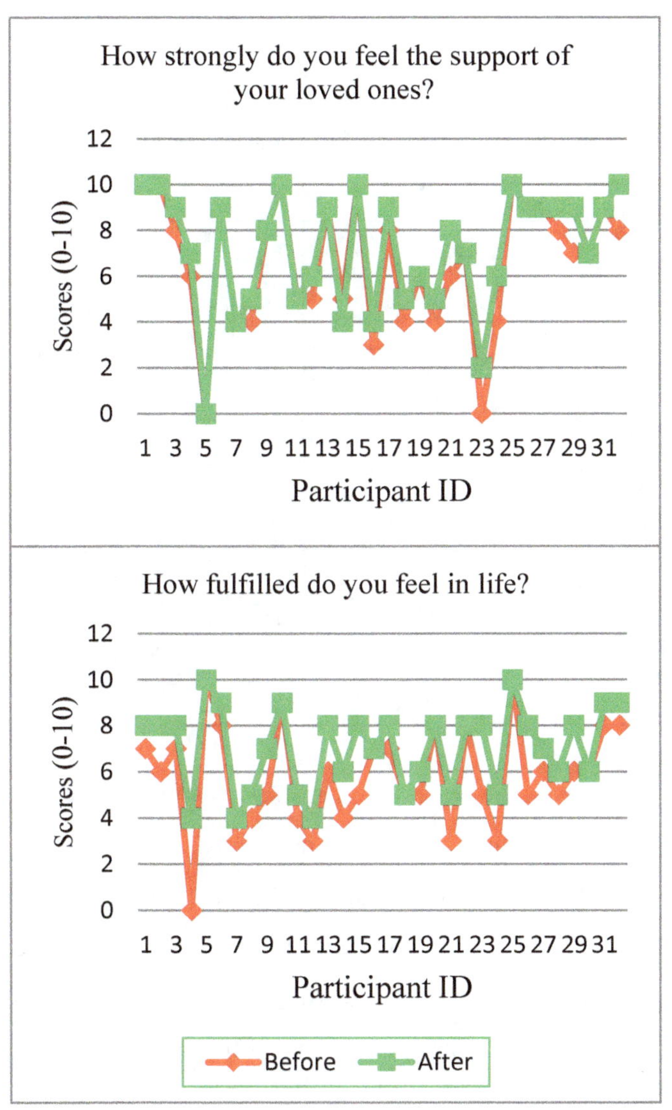

How strongly do you feel the support of your loved ones?
Scores (0-10)
12
10
8
6
4
2
0
1 3 5 7 9 11 13 15 17 19 21 23 25 27 29 31
Participant ID
How fulfilled do you feel in life?
Scores (0-10)
12
10
8
6
4
2
0
1 3 5 7 9 11 13 15 17 19 21 23 25 27 29 31
Participant ID
Before
After

Summary table of the minimum, maximum values, sum, and average of the answers before and after completing the program.

	Question 1 (Anxiety)	Question 2 (Sleep)	Question 3 (Uncertainty)	Question 4 (Support)	Question 5 (Fulfillment)
Minimum value BEFORE	5	0	1	0	0
Minimum value AFTER	3	0	1	0	4
Maximum value BEFORE	10	10	10	10	10
Maximum value AFTER	8	9	9	10	10
Sum BEFORE	234	199	200	212	186
Sum AFTER	179	157	179	230	226
Average value BEFORE	7,3	6,2	6,3	6,6	5,8
Average value AFTER	5,6	4,9	5,6	7,2	7,0

From the constructed graphs and summary table, we can draw the following conclusions:

1. There is a significant improvement in the dynamics, with decreased levels of anxiety, sleep problems, and fear of the unknown. Additionally, there is an increase in the perception of support and personal fulfillment.

2.	The minimum level of anxiety, before the program, was 5, which decreased to 3 after completing the program.

3.	The maximum level of anxiety also decreased, from 10 before the program to 8 after.

4.	The overall sum of anxiety scores decreased by 55 points, from 234 to 179.

5.	The average score also decreased by 1.7 points, from 7.3 to 5.6.

6.	The maximum level of sleep problems decreased from 10 to 9.

7.	The overall sum of sleep problem scores decreased by 42 points, from 199 to 157.

8.	The average score also decreased by 1.7 points, from 7.3 to 5.6.

9.	The maximum level of fear of the unknown decreased from 10 to 9.

10.	The overall sum decreased by 21 points, from 200 to 179.

11.	The average score decreased by 0.7 points, from 6.3 to 5.6.

12.	The perception of support among program participants increased by 18 points, from 212 to 230 in total.

13.	The average score increased from 6.6 to 7.2, by 0.6 points.

14.	The minimum score for the sense of personal fulfillment increased from 0 to 4.

15.	The maximum score increased from 5.8 to 7.0, by 1.2 points.

The positive dynamics after completing the three-week program independently are evident.

CONCLUSIONS

According to the goals and objectives, research was conducted with the participation of men and women aged 25 to 40. There were 27 women and 5 men among the participants, making a total of 32 people in the study. To achieve this goal, the following tasks were accomplished:

1. A clear understanding of the criteria that constitute the concept of "personality" was formed.

2. The specificity of art therapy as a method in psychotherapy was examined.

3. The potential for applying art therapy methods to develop internal support in individuals was determined.

4. A set of art therapy exercises aimed at developing internal support in clients was developed.

5. An experimental study was conducted with a control group.

6. The results were collected and analyzed.

Conclusions were drawn about the work done. In the first chapter, a research hypothesis was developed:

we hypothesized that if a series of art therapy exercises aimed at creating internal support in individuals is developed and applied in practice, we will observe an increase in the indicators of internal support and a reduction in stress and anxiety levels in the control group. This hypothesis was fully confirmed. The indicators for each stated item improved. The highest improvement dynamics were observed in the "anxiety" category.

Individual completion of art therapy exercises has proven its value in developing internal supports, which are crucial in life. Internal supports are internal resources that help us cope with life's challenges, build healthy relationships, manage stress, and achieve our goals.

Through its creative and expressive nature, art therapy allows participants to explore and develop their internal supports. By visualizing their thoughts, emotions, and achievements, participants create symbolic images that represent their strengths, values, and resources. This helps them become aware of and strengthen their inner confidence, self-efficacy, and self-expression.

The development of internal supports is a key aspect of personal growth and well-being. When we have internal supports, we feel more balanced, adaptable, and capable of overcoming difficulties. Art therapy provides participants with the opportunity to expand their self-understanding, discover new sources of strength, and cultivate a more positive attitude towards themselves and their lives.

Thus, art therapy is an effective tool for developing internal supports that play a vital role in our lives, contributing to our psychological and emotional well-being.

Literature

1. Kopytin, A.I. Modern clinical art therapy: A textbook. - M.: Kogito-Center, 2015.

2. Malkiodi, K. Palette of the soul. The transformative power of art: the path to health and well-being. - K.: "Sofia"; M.: Publishing house "Sofia", 2004.

3. Malchiodi, K. Creativity and the brain // Art therapy - new horizons / Edited by A.I. Kopytin. - M.: Kogito-Center, 2006.

4. Psychology of states: Textbook / Edited by A.O. Prokhorov. - M.: Publishing house "Kogito-Center", 2011.

5. Rubin, D. A. The Art of art therapy. - M.: Publishing house "Institute of General Humanitarian Research", 2015.

6. Hulbut, G. Taming the storm: intermodal art therapy as a tool overcoming feelings of anger and shame in patients who have suffered emotional trauma // Art therapy in the postmodern era / Edited by A.I. Kopytin. - St. Petersburg: "Speech", "Semantics-C", 2002.

7. Schaverien, J. The revealing image: analytical art psychotherapy in theory and practice. - L., Philadelphia: Jessica Kingsley Publishers, 1999.